OTHER BOOKS BY THE AUTHOR

MYSTERIES

Wall of Darkness
The Eternity Look
Domino
The Sweat Box
Under Dragon House
Blueprint
Snapshot, Collected Stories
Rope
Trojan Park
Border

POETRY

Cherished Memory
(Poems & A Play)

PSYCHOLOGY
Social Work From A Therapeutic Perspective

*D*amascus *R*ose

J. Lea Koretsky

REGENT PRESS
Berkeley, California

Copyright © 2012 by Judy Koretsky

[paperback]
ISBN 13: 978-1-58790-230-7
ISBN 10: 1-58790-230-3

[e-book]
ISBN: 13: 978-1-58790-231-4
ISBN 10: 1-58790-231-1

Library of Congress Control Number: 2012957804

Manufactured in the U.S.A.

REGENT PRESS
Berkeley, California
www.regentpress.net

Contents

Wave Crashers	1
Farrago	3
Interlude	5
Mast Poles	6
Long At Love	7
Tie My Bow	8
Evasion	9
Tricked Out	10
Enchant	12
Into the Tide	14
Make Some Noise	15
Suck Eggs	17
Cancan	17
Only Discontent	18
In All Aspects of Living	19
Love Defined	20
Bold Seduction	22
Commitment	24
Madness	25
Rush	27
Bismarck Atoll	28
Attentive Observation	30
Gamble	31
Blue	32
Casino Waitress	33
Violet Winter	35
Ocean Wave	36
Killing Sleep	37
Crumpet and Tea	38
Museum Art	39
Mama's Royal Café	40
Geomorphic Moon	41
Incurable Romance	42

A Day at the Lake	43
Performa	44
Night Life	45
Puerta	46
Winter's Lamp	47
Salt Lake City Going Home	50
Cachet	54
Winter Song	55
Winter Equinox	57
Centerpiece	58
A Feast of Apples	59
Train from Quebec City to Noval Scotia	60
Blowing Glass at the Harbor	63
What Is Known	65
Leaving At Night	66
50 Pesos	67
In the Field of Rustling Grasses	68
From a Stand of Walnut Trees	69
Aptos, California	70
Recollections of Arabstar and Mir	72
Plain on the Moon's Surface	74
Horizon	76
Quick Turns	78
Haute Couture	81
Russian Ships on the Sea	82
Two in the Morning, Ryer's Island	83
Spring	85
Summer	86
Winter	91
Imprints	95
El Escritorio	97
Discipline	102
Damascus Rose	104

WAVE CRASHERS

Colony of rooks of battlements
A discography –
An assemblage
Of ocean recordings
Overcrowd, jam
Dilutions
In an uproar
Like combat between fighter aircraft
Echoes resound
All surface ice on water
Anthologize
Into a corundum, abrasive
Crackle like paintwork patterned with minute surface
    cracks.
Creases in the cream blench;
Left open, the jar is
A cretaceous cranny
A chink, a crimp;
In a second gaps
Of scattered debris
Form a likeness of
Crayfish teeming
Deranged, flaky, avid
Madly obsessed
Like crinoline crinkling
Underwater, a serpentine curtain
Nebulous or inscrutable.

A shout flashes on the spittle of wind
Like a handle of a whip
In a decisive moment of dependency
The crew repress

The bridle to gauge
An unmerciful savagely relentless
Assault of winds
A high ocean denunciation
Derailed by a violent typhoon
Driving downpour
Demeaned by impaired reasoning
The dementia of storm fury
One's stubborn subordinate
Pretensions of the calling of the sea
Precarious dear life
Swindled by will or lease
Interminable impatience
Or docile submission –
Sails like quivering wings
On drift nets
At draft depth
To float a ship.

Farrago

Merriment, conviviality
A chain of eucalyptus leaves
Adorned with gold ribbons
Flamenco, plumed flamingo dancers
Joie de vivre in ballroom mirrors
When the vase containing
Small fragrant white flowers
Cracks –
A farrago of chaos, fright, insensate despair
Arises out of breaking news
Becomes a desperate calamity
Irrevocably lost
Nothing valid, justified, equitable
Junkies in the junkyard
Kimono kite
Hopeless finality
Intolerable intrusion
Jigsaw
Garish, tawdry discord
Bright yellow forsythia
Caught in delicate gossamer spider webs
A gown of granulate iridescent rayon
An indulgence
A grandiosity of sugary guano
Gelatinous intoxicating conceit
Haughtier pride
Exhilaration before jingo
Weighty secrets the way sheaths sparkle
Confining hem
Crusty heel of contempt
Hellebore Christmas rose
Hemlock its own hemoglobin

After a helical fashion
Faltering heterodox
Hermetic hiding place
Gastropod
Wrecking injury
Tied up by a Gorgon
To a slay bed
Bloodied and clotted
Rich coagulated cheese
With blue veins
Useless
Reduced
Inhospitable future
Crippling contusions
Intercede, please, with prayer

Interlude

An adaptation to
Living alone
A series of warbling calls
Lingers awhile
Hear the kingfisher's laughing cry
Be affable but keep me
Through intercessions
By design or purpose
Reciprocally essential
Like the black liquid ejected by a cuttlefish
Imprinting judicial law
Into submissive dissolutions
Troubleshooter or pleader
Chocolate mint colophon or virgin lime
Astringent wines of tangerine and grapefruit
Ephemeral daylight
With diversions
Like hanging racemes
Violet wind dashes over the windowpane
A host of white zebras,
So many they stampede
In diagonal dust whirlwinds
While we eat wolfishly
Slightly drunk on curry and melon condiment
A rarity of phenomenon
A hurrah whipped from wind.

Mast Poles

The line pulls tight –
Choppy waves buck a red boat
Mount it on a crest;
A child holding his mother's hand
As he pulls her impatiently
Along the pier
Points –
"Look! Look!
The boat is rocking!"

The mast poles in the quay
Make a line of defense
To looming clouds
Lowering onto the lake,
The waves retort ascending
Whipper-in soaking the sandy beach
In sudden rain, wind a faint sound
"A wibble-wabble!
The dock is leaving!"

Long at Love

Intangible spice condiment obsessed
Either salty or sugary
Long at love
Is all that matters
In a kitchen with two of everything;
Indecent white cake dressed
In icy sugary frosting sits on a shelf
I for one only want below zero nights
The two of us beneath the quilts
A small heat pad between us.
Insatiable moments require no less
Pneumatic weather, littoral strand
As long as I can be near you
Plunge into your spring-tide
Clamor for your clime.

Tie My Bow

I'm in a hurry, babe
Tie my bow
I'm passion at the wheel, babe
Load my stow
I'm stepping out to a show, babe
Whip my machismo
I'm desiring you on my arm, babe
Stag my sparrow
We'll have a fine time, love
Be my Pernod.

I'm leaving real soon, babe
You sit on my palomino
I'm going down south, babe
You bend my arrow
I'm buying a farm, babe
Girl, let's fly to de Janeiro
I'm doing this right, babe
Tying you up in my bolero
We'll shoot for the stars, sweetheart
Be my Monte Carlo.

Precious you are to me, babe
Be my glow, girl
Sum of perfection, babe
Habituate my crescendo
I want you for a lifetime, babe
Melt in my kino
Take you to the justice, babe
Wear my bingo
Swear to you no other, I love you
Be my ultimo.

Evasion

If I be less than what you would have liked
Could I at least implore of you my wit
Mischief faultless detests its mean catch spiked
Accursed deficiency ransom permit;
Were you to learn the depth of my appeal
Thousand pardons you might enjoy revise
While I deny the labyrinth quest a seel
Nature invokes winter mistruths subside;
Were I spinster, old maid or fool tenure
Had I banished men's affection a sting
Delicate green and fine linen wise lure
Too much a joy to bask in sequence cling;
Reciprocal combat yields to essences
Your favors, my overindulgences.

Tricked Out

Schizophrenia is all bluster
there's enmity
it's not on speaking terms
discord insolence brash
sometimes deadly quiet
asks if they like him

mania on the other hand is a motor
the mouth is always going
speech is staccato, adamant
out of the question he feels good
would rather talk fast enough
to hyperventilate –
maintains control all the way
to the inauguration

and then paranoid trait
the type won't open up
sulks, keeps a distance
a prig on purpose
what d'ya want?
I gave you my fucking name

dopers exist in dualities
their agonies and angst
are stage effects
punct-o, strut, pomp
snubb-ed, submissive
okay, man! whatever you say
daddio, aspire me an idol

let's be garish, tricked out
anxiety pushing a que
roll up the words with marbles

spit them out, persecuted
afflicted, abhorrent, piteous
let's hug ourselves, lament
agonize indignant, let's be tricked

Enchant

Love me
Indulge
Gratify
Amuse
Please
Be
Cheeky
Saucy
Pert
Glittering
A tart
Find me
In whimsy
Wide hat awake
Wide of distance
Verging to
Reaching within an arc
At the threshold
Of your nearness
For keeping
Provide a tente d'abri
A galoche and spatter-dash
A coma to a flood-gate
Speed! as to slack
Port of departure
Advise
Dissuade me
From impulse
Out of drenching rain
Out of biting icy cold
With remedy
Into asylum, the storm blown over
To a toxicology of morphine
Into safe harbor

Belladonna sublimate
Depression tenable en deshabille
Too much leisure, a laboring oar
Compass astray
Embrace me
Recruit reciprocity
Love me
Gratify
Indulge

Into the Tide

Deferring is not resignation
Any more than being humble is a capitulation
Turning the other cheek
Is not suffering decision
Nor making the best of it
As a disputant or polemic.

A sporting flotilla emerges from the leaves
Heavy dragoon of mounted telescopes
Tourists watching for slithering alligators
Peon sepoy beneath wide basket hat at the wheel
Scrawny arms turning franc-tireur
Into the tide of an inflamed setting sun
Searchlights blaring, first line of defense.

The brush comes alive with birds
Belting light, neon blue ricochets on the fiber glass windows
Below which we crouch aware only of passing sprigs overhead
Praying the boat will drift swiftly through still waters
The sudden freaky wail of a flying prehistoric bird
Clinches the air at a dizzying height.

Watching the boundary for renegades
Silence between rounds specifies the start of triumph
To remain in possession of the field
Ropes of squawking rooster cages hanging from trees
A deaf ear to renunciations and disclaimers
An incantation of supplication vouchsafes for the unconditional
It is the vow of observance.

Make Some Noise

Let's have a run
Come into style
Be sought after
Hold a halo
Flaunt our laurels
Cut a figure.

We'll make some noise
Have a party, blow a reamer
Take our degree
Obtain our masters
Be talk of the town
Elevate our status.

He will make a great card
She will land constellations
The oldest will win at math
The second acquire an honor
The third raise his head
A family of pink pearls in ascent.

I'll be a hero
You can be a lion
I'll have éclat
You success and prestige
We'll paint the town
Shine in our popularity.

We'll make a big splash
Vie with our smart friends
Boast our immortality
Establish our authority
It'll be glorious
Life will be stupendous.

SUCK EGGS

You don't have to admit it
You're a saucy pert,
I don't have to agree
To take a liberty.

You might be a puff
A boast and a bluff,
I might be a crow
Keep you company
Be free and easy.

CANCAN

From the loge the theatre revives
Lights dim to chaste garnet
Cancan like pink, rust and red carnations
All tinsel, across the stage dagger between his lips
A male troubadour all black sequins
Banter dapper
Showy radiance around a pistil
Frolic for enchantment;

He clicks his heels
Raises his hands, claps
Petticoats rustle, ole
With tap dancing staccato
The pink and rust carnation
Slides to the wing.

Only Discontent

No regrets, only discontent
Cheered from time to time
Consoled for a whimper,
I could not forget
When the birch were bound
By cinch or those exiled
To a howling wilderness
Where virulent blue takes Man's mortal soul –
His ephemeral anthropology,
His instantaneity, a plurality of moments
At once a unity
And an epoch
Like granules

Plumed feathers, each having an eye
Weighty portends of regal dress
A mannequin stepping cautiously
Monotonous pedestrian
Cymbals clanging
Peculiar, aberrant, frayed
Despite weakly euphoric exhilaration
The adversary, dissonance
Edgy hostility, jittery, restless mettle

Hibiscus petals scattered in the wind
Ignominy pronounced
A coastward clutch
Mist a misprint or misunderstanding
Obscuring glass to the soft gray-green
Pastel of the new saplings it reflects

In All Aspects of Living

In all aspects of living
Just the one disappointment
No moment ever returns
It expands into universes

Unlike water which contracts
Shrinks from its life-salving essence
To the merest pocket of rock
Illusory reflection, green film on bronze

The ephemeral, the fleeting
As incidental as infatuation
As a heartthrob is to martyrdom
As obsession is to a crush

Come form me, instruct me
Split the space into parts
Be obsessive, esoteric
Paint until sunrise, tempest at midnight

My life has faded just a sharp note
Too jarring, an antagonist
Of baffling syndromes
Each sound its own ontogeny

My circle of posies falling downwind
Collects in my skirt like a chain.

Love Defined

Ideal cupid sorely finds a flight
Light speed a whip invents no clouds for noon
Love simpler in revel doth expedite
Clear path with pleasure found may practice soon;
If the subject ne'er lets on so keen complaint
Nor leaves a book of poems for her to know
The hour that passion could imbue finds faint
As oars across the lake impart a row;
Condensed may be a kind acquaintance start
Beguiling looks have oft' kept compliment
Enjoy so tender possession of heart
Design the world in pairs rejoice portent;
Can two apart intend as one alit
Of love most bourne contend a favor writ?
Of course the subject has no false retort
Does plainly seem accord in all replies
Could easily invent the mischief of tort
If daring carefree whimsy makes denies;
That ardor craves a straight forward receipt
Understands truth as Nature most divine
Escapes to holidays for poems discreet
Wanders afar rejoiced the two entwine;
In practice long the plait doth draw the braid
Holiness in white shuns gossip's tongues in ink
Prayer in pews arranges life terms made
That two must oar as one in measured sync;
Any query must address Love's habit
To believe design a favorable rennet.
Should death intrude like Romeo's chaste Juliet
Were life spent dear a price would ne'er afford
To make whimsy seem fooled mischief comic
Desire measured complaint borrows reward;

The woes of dirges afloat on Tirius convey
All cynicism displayed by masks conjured
Dwarfed duty like foamy fog array
Commitment like anointment sculpt amour;
Mature overture wise infantry adore
Long coveted epigraph inscribes envy
Merry absinthe acquaints intrusive mentor
To such idea sleep holds no generosity;
Into the River Lethe masks must submerge
Constellations like stars from depths emerge.
True love has no ignoble task partake
No false release from query's merry chase
No matter under how many skies he ache
One undoing constitutes a lover's phase;
Were love described easy as spring's warm day
Had she numbered sparrows around her dress
The pure would make so fine a bed au fait
Long night delirium an enchanted arrest;
Beguiling trysts in pale moonlight allure
Although soft words bespake a chime ascend
The nearest brush a touch restraint endure
Until advice improve a mirror's friend.
On a maxim wit disguise doth displease
Discus lectern agreed compose its ease.

Bold Seduction

Fitting bodice and tight waistband disarm
The die are thrown in eager devotion
Crafty devise bequeath approved charm
Resolute sense surrenders fine emotion;
Devious deviling devise detour
Impairment decides all outcomes unknown
Elements corrupt reveal cynosure
Descent into underworld rotenone;
Forsake those derelict and deputy
Catch sight of deception fake or in hock
Cornucopia of glinting confetti
Excess carnal décolleté defrock;
Elusive good seeks its tender hauteur
Insouciant custom a brave voyageur.
Damask rose like splendid Dahlia exalt
Perfume that emasculates zeal endows
Love in its heart doth prove erstwhile gestalt
Meanwhile Miranda in glass slipper glows;
The New World from arctic peak epoch
Ice floes in greenest velvet gowns astride
Epiphany epistle springs lovelock
Equable streams wind all the way to tide;
For this engendered affections promise
A stable lad with pulse a race solo
Fleshy prerogative peeked nakedness
Andante prince primrose posts to polo;
Exquisite veil threshold doth win at love
Romance plummet gratefully mends the glove.
Wonderment at insights glamour reply
Instinctual and seductive possum
Idyllic crux an arbutus dulcify
Breezes nor draught demise untamed autumn;
Honey flowers in abundance on vines

Sweeten arable adventure raison
Intoxicating droll, miraculous lines
Sentient preambles bold strike emblazon;
Oh greenery! A mystic courts true love
Divination truth captures image
Scent defies all warning wine clove
Geese flying south honk alarming steerage;
Femme boughs with ribbons tied to sweetest clasp
Endear only virile steed with wise gasp.
Beloved, awake, implore your staid wisdom
Signify you accept humblest virtue
Gardens abloom with visions of Nasturtiums
Showy hollyhock picturesque value;
Implement a doodle and count the stars
Say good morning and kiss your life husband
Give thanks to lawn and hanging tire antiar
Expire the thought Scylla sings for marooned;
M'lady, ditch the sled and preen the sail upwind
Travel by scull onto the snowbound lake
Clamber wind cliffs with springy step sequined
The smallest balm releases sincere heartache;
No matter how far your ship tends your sail
Only your image stakes for yearning's tale.
Sands run through your hourglass melancholy
Good manners before confession
Make the subject worthy of love's monopoly
For Mercy's insatiable obsession;
Once charitable indulgent talent
More refined than graceful finesse wed
Rapt endearments educate merriment
Narcotic thwarted indictment misled;
Pastimes are plenty gird despite brocade
Finest costume doth wear a bib too soon
Age knows never a shade or bridie glade
Despite weather bestows privy cocoon;
Love held close gives consummate paragon
Faultless perfection brow completes stollen.

Commitment

A whistle at the break of dawn disposes
Glorious sun behind branches arise
Carefree charmed whims caprice wicked willows
Into his arms the breath winter surprise;
The lake final freezes opaque grey blue
All sentiment lavish enthralling joy
Before snowflakes dispel doves cry lasso
Miscue shallow fissures leafy ducks decoy;
Had he provocation impulse overcome
The stars of heaven show like falling dew
Habitual addiction pays its plum
Precious softness prevails for aim's rood;
Across the ice as blue and green salchow
Timed ballerinas to jump aikido.
Are we but placed on earth for chance and love
Boulevardier Tenzing Norgay weaned lure
Does Life break through charcoal dust ink for trove
Draw mist onto mount painting scrolls to stir;
Must call derive from echoes far to tempt
Convention fall toward bait seasoned habit
Quarrel forbidden wants and perceive empt
Like any teen who recants boned rarebit;
Eventually motive runs a rut
Spirits arouse hunger and force raison
From solitude rhapsodic output
Taproot beetroot permutes a liaison;
Diet as proof comforts the lovers root
Certain pursuit doth aid enhanced resolute.

Madness

To rise to occasion yet lose the vogue
Adhere true love affection's bewitching hour
Persuade the spicy dram of habit's yoke
Induce religion from the brine dower;
Sturdy chilled winds abide the blind stiff damp
The cuckoo bird disorients its mate
Shutters windows at draft to blur the lamp
Find rage deviation advantage late;
The haw-haw crows his tune a tired excuse
Low laid schemes play to chords cacophonous
Wired screech harrows anxious tight reduce
Even though bright or dull tunes chaos;
Any cycle of eclipses on Paros
Greek island foretold albatross rimose.
A jarring deduction which clamors douse
A stalking horse given into remorse
Male in essence controlled by joint recluse
White buds cover barren foothills fore course;
On the Aegean Sea hundreds of sails stand wind
Knowledge herself doth keep a trade of clay
She wails in spite of taciturn rescinds
And recreational forced labor émigré;
A woman loved by a dominate hand
Forbids herself cymar and speckled jewel
Always love lies on ocean counted sand
Each hour reducing leaves no trace of duel;
Just this, mistrust conjures fairest raw silk
The gilded pill the breath pulls short Love's ilk.
No spillway leads a voyageur to tide
Although sun torched wanderers see
An ocean flowing o'er sand dunes confide
Dates and caviar are all nomads feed;

Scarcity defines the hungry soul's eye
Irrational exhaust depletes ample
Exuberant poverty frisks Bourbon wry
Enlist for want imports ready upheaval;
How doth mystical love surrender still?
That all the world purpose directs one's heart
Should love readily insist on force of will
Or constitute for able men matched part?
Shall Life be reckless yet to sights untamed
Unworthy keep a portal to shores named?
Isle of seasons fair doth mark trade winds
Afloat hearty sailors stay trim on top
Keenest sure foot reckons rope masts find fins
The double waits ashore in crates of crop;
Decipher's interpret meaning of truth
While hands fetch ale for slop barstool hour
Partners pair up by two for ends of soothe
Remiss of how many quaint tabs go dour;
Distraught acquittals test the heart forlorn
Leave yet feckless rails below the currents
Astern to ports of love a captain's dorn
Much less legal distress deterrents;
To endless isles in search of perfect love
For troves of keepsake who wan at coves.

Rush

Rush, rush
Be a caw, caw
Pillar, pillar
Be a raven crow
Wind, wind
Be a knockabout
Tempest wind
Be a soaring whistle
Phosphorescent light over the marsh

Wind sleeve
Be a quarrel, quarrel
Crank up, up
Rush, rush
Be a caw, caw
An agitating crow
Be a zephyr, be a squall
Come at nine, green
Tree beginnings protruding through low water

Rush, rush
Be a caw, caw
A scarecrow, a raven
Wind, wind

BISMARCK ATOLL

No one hears the rock slide
Underwater as it cascades heavily
A wretched hillside rilled by creeping mud
All weight, fauna and locker wood heave on chains
Gradually increasing in loudness
A twirl of dim light scarps off coral ledges
Small lobsterlike crustaceans release in a tizzy.
From the robot cage
Mechanical light arm extends
Into a conviction of utter darkness,
Above a fifty mile reef atoll
A half mile tar sand in vivid light blue becomes
A crescent doctoring on the flat ocean expanse
Turquoise skeletal bones rising from the open sea
150 North, 5 West bound by the Bismarck
Geode composition seen only by air.
Like lustrous fiber produced by a silkworm
Algae coagulates with granules
Becomes submerged, eventually spreads out
Sinecure and distinct, deposit box bar
Umbrellas, beach chairs, oceanfront or poolside
Poker hand with three of a kind and a pair
A hundred thousand lambs from satellite image
In dead of winter waves stiffen and harden
For months they are immobilized in shallow water
Further out at sea the serpent's tail switches.
The bronze mist which rises inland in valleys
Pours down steep mountain verdure slopes
Scintillating in rivulets onto the ocean at dawn
Captures the nets of fishermen who stand in boats
Cast gray webs in spinning motion
Weighted by copper balls onto the bay

Dredge the misty waters of eel, brine, goby.
When the celestial orbit exhibits wrap up
He will go back to Germany and do the same exhibit there
Leave a pattern of scarecrow beneath the snow
From an arrogant distance
If he's not in a consumptive mind
He will read Sarte, study Pinter or anyone who's the bet
Wait for art to conjure
For diadromous ice to show climate change;
He's a tragic man from way back when
Son of the late Sixties, early Seventies,
When even listening to Janis Joplin was a sin of omission
When riding a curl on a surfboard was cool Man, awesome
And beneath the surface a thousand magenta striped
    yellow fish
Swam out of pink coral reef as though through castle
    windows
At the Chinese café.

Attentive Observation

Mathematics for the ratio of the cotangent
No such thing as holism
There's content, size, limit
Sprightly son in jodhpurs with whip
Sits on eggs as though to brood on a horse
Jejune yet intoxicating
A stir of imminent breeze
Flight of far-fetching physics
To a traversable emotional release
Eighteenth century Reason and Individualism
Magi Epiphanies
Moments of intense unqualified insight
Of polemic, visionary deep motivation
Prodigal scholarship
Ceremonial aestheticism
Mutual reciprocity
Platonic allegories
Rigorously precise distinct from Mind and Spirit
Miraculous medicine.

Gamble

Mournful in the mouth
Aimless drifter
Life's a lottery
An impractical gamble

Life's a worry, an escape
Could be detached
One is more secure
Looks like rain
Ominously close

Wouldn't trust the looks of a dead ringer
Spitting image of a demand of instructions
Destiny's a bitch and Fate a harbinger
A watch not tightly held is a curl in the wind

Scorn one's temper, disdain
The straw one draws
Karma is a liniment, fortune
Its own object

Disengage and let go
Bet at long odds, linger idle
Make a long jump
Try for success due to chance

Oh, I'm totally in love with a good cup of coffee.

BLUE

Venetian blind summer mornings
The bed attired by an all white comforter, white sheets and two pillows
In the sitting room on the beige berber only a single chair
Which is white

A melancholia
Blue
All things being equal, white says more
Blue conjures up distance, conservative leanings
Stolid prominence

Whereas in sunlight white fades
There is no lack of fascination
Of the endless open sea
Omniscient no matter the strength of sun

Photostat in blue
Twigs and leaves reproduce with radiant light
As though they must be stars and nebulae
Phylum of phylogeny

White of course is the juice of the poppy
Medicinal opium or a porter stout rich in saccharine
Divine prescience, opinion narcotic
Blue hyacinth stands by itself, until it dies
White as a Hyades.

Casino Waitress

Like an omen of one's unpleasant fate
Stuffed bananas soaked in absinthe
Perception, quick and discriminating
Rises above azo dye to leave a benzidene stain
As strong as a conjou tea might be congruent.

You have yearned for long-marinated fruit
Sweetened to scarcely visible lemon rind
Delicacy of brief remembered joys and virtue
Of one's conceit as durable as any computation.
I have merely a singular compulsion
An agnostic commiseration to be left alone
Despite the belief that a collimate shall set life straight
And order, once established, will bring conformity.

I awaken in the thick of night concerned
That I have indulged, yet neglected lenience
Feeling that I have lived past my prime
I content myself with finger crab cakes, soda biscuit
Stodgy caviar paste on celery, hazelnut fig crèmes
It's a choice to sit beneath one's covered porch
In the path of the fan, the wind stirring about
Sip melon spice, nibble pastry, and forget the stuff
Of which disappointments create a sting of regret.

Lu Ella, Lu Ella, why don't you swish your velvet skirt
    my way
Lu Ella, Lu Ella, why don't you bend
Give yourself a reason, give your glance astray
Take my breath a pause, make me a brilliant ray
Lu Ella, Lu Ella, why won't you bring your tray
A spoon of honey, a bouquet of thyme, lilac sachet

Mend my wicked thoughts, send my cares away
Oh, loose your stepping tight matinee
Ride bareback on my jet black mare on the highway
Crimson petticoats and silk raw orange leggings flyaway
Lu Ella, Lu Ella, why won't you,
Why won't you, lass,
Cover me a waistcoat and in my sleep be a Hathaway
Oh, Lu Ella, Lu Ella, why don't you sway your high bizet
Why won't you bend, steer my heart astray?

Violet Winter

The end of the marriage
Minced by acrimonious blame
And Sybille warnings
Becomes a violet winter
In which neurotic undertones
Are perjured
By lachrymose expression.
Forward, forward
Time contradicts
Before it moves ahead.

Ocean Wave

Billowing silk as blue
As an ocean wave
Reveals itself to be
Luxuriant sapphire blue
And also blissful gulf stream
Artistic aquamarine;

Only a delightful breeze
Is resistant to patterns
Of grey rain.

Pale powder blue streamers
Like open-mouthed fish
Gape in the force
Of a froth-flying squall
Esoteric banners of sailcloth
Restrained against the fighting pressure
Of the rippling chill.

Golden ocean water gleams
On the pasty chalk beach
Strewn with driftwood
Which the ocean has hurtled
From the cacophony of its depths.

In the bay a man
Dressed in a dark wetsuit
Wind surfs, his taut sail
Yellow and white with a pink stripe
Is whipped stiff by the wind.

Killing Sleep

Irascible psyche
Talk to me
About mundane denials
Lustily driven love
Minor pertinences
Or moody reverence
Soiled by less than holy
Joinings.

Mildew like curdled milk
Morbid speckled frost
The damp a deadly killing
Worse than a ransom –
Hopeful entendres
Given insufficient nurturance
Instructs chill during a rostrum
Of impotent pleas
Cribs all air
In suffocation
As when marsh succumbs
To its coal.

Were it not
For the coachman's whip
To hasten the parents' lament
A child would be killed
By the kindness of ether
Or mucus.

Crumpet and Tea

Holiday in the sitting room
Tiny white lights on tall round bush trees
Carpet of white gooseberry and flocked snow
Ministry of snowflakes falling to earth
Carols of merriment, harmonious tidings
Twinkling joy fill the night
While down the chimney marshal Rudolph
And a sled of deer and careful antlers.
Dad runs to fetch the children
Before the snowman loses its cap
A ride down the hill on a board
All three bundled up with bells
To the bottom frozen pond,
Back inside for hot cider
And hanging the silver icing
Gold leaves of poinsettas
Ribbons and tassles and stars.

Museum Art

having examined from a perspective
how to wander in imagination to create
a true contemplation of sorrow
I sit on a bench in a museum
glancing periodically at grey snow
minimal jots of thought tried at any angle
to lose self-conscious divorce
wedge a half avocado between
a grapefruit slice
and an egg
inside an elongated building of white rooms
each with a narrow black door inviting a student
perform a bass concerto in C minor
heavy sonorous relief
in droplets of a cold shower
releasing full on a stultifying day
an indescribable prickling sensation.

Mama's Royal Café

while outside in a pre-ten o'clock downpour
at the breakfast joint on Broadway it's standing room
only for the jalapeno eggs
four waitresses from the Midwest wearing salmon
aprons in blue tennis
carrying trays with hot dust bowl oats, black strap and
cashew pumpkin bread
esteemable ginger and sweet potato pancakes
emerge from a green and pink tile kitchen through
swinging double doors
to ugly green booths where customers sip double
espressos
and draw napkin art featured in Sunday's local news
every March
the manager's profile in red against a dark brown accent
wall and the restaurant's cacti garden,
the luxurious living room entry of wine sofas, posh
bench mirrors for coats,
opaque glass between the eating counter and tables
jogger's aloe vera and crushed yarrow in tall frosted
glasses
weekend chef grilling lobster flambé during finals
making weiner dogs out of thin light green and orange
balloons
every breakfast a festive romantic notion

Geomorphic Moon

Spike-lets of finch, swallow, seagull
Fossil cretaceous marine spiny wings
Trapped in clay and mud
Hundreds of wings
A hymnal ground
For henotheism.

In a feeding frenzy
A flapping clamor
A liturgical monadic jeering skirmish
Wildly thrashing madness
Frantic bath for the gardyloo
From a distance a genocide
Seen at a glim of sparkling water
Above a mercurial river through carpetweed
Savage slaughter of golden shiner fish

Unrestrained shrieking
Like a fervid hysteria
Of heretical hoodoos gone horn-mad.
To hear it, sharp querulous rebukes
Which sounds disintegrate
For morsels, scraps or a sliver
Gluttonous plutocracy
Thrashing intolerant purgatory.

INCURABLE ROMANCE

Rosary pea, orange lucweed
Dogbane, wild blue lobelia
Indicant blue vat dye
Indifferent indigence
Indissoluble indulgence
Perpetual inkblot
Prize profligate emotion
Red integration
Image given back
Refulgent
All life is reincarnated.

A Day at the Lake

Necks float on the lake
Hail dive bombs the water
Geese fight to have a piece
Yokes –
A carp jumps into air
An energetic leap for such a young thing
Geese honk flapping as they run up the grass.

Preforma

Dispassionate embrace
Sincure philandering
Humanitarian woe
Stravage, strop
To bait one's malice on
The artless nature of a man
Who prides himself a gangue
The way the gander sits for months on the eggs
To smother them
With overt antagonism
A nested mutton
Sealed with too much moisture
Frothy parturition
They aren't even good for eating
Sinister prodigal waste
Puerile fascination
Frugal parsimony.

Night Life

Night life sizzling drum beat
Flamingo ruffled skirts
Carnation crepe Charleston rhumba dresses
Pink, green, yellow light and dark pastels
Mexican luxury

Dash of heavy rain off
A jet blue ocean
Sky carpeted by a monsoon
Turns into a bag of sunshine
An hour before sunset

Quick! From the lounge door spills out
Tambourine and wailing throaty singer
Platinum blonde stiff curls
In slinky silver sequins
Fox fur wrap white shoulders

She makes a run for it
Through light rain
Glistening street, follow that cab
Light green and dark brown checker
She's on cue, a smile for the photo journalist.

Puerta

Cobbled stone, high plaza wall along the battering coast
A pungent aroma of nutmeg bushes delights

Below, ships course through the harbor
Icy aqua blue water

Wharf edges stacked with yellow flounder
And crimson floor stones

My plate has slices of oranges and cinnamon spiced pumpkin
Demitasse and walnut-stuffed dates.

The white tablecloth flaps in a sudden wind
Light blue glass plates and frosted margaritas

Silver backed chilled herring with dill weed
Sea shells litter the sand path

Clairvoyant voices at sea
Come tumbling in with each pounding wave

The grey rain streaked fence
Rests afar the old fashioned lighthouse

The quilt of purple and blue squares
That lies across my lap keeps out the chill.

Winter's Lamp

1.
Swollen snowflakes out of a windy scattering sky disperse
Gold sprinkled glittering pinecones and firm orange red persimmons
Fill a basket punctuated by pungent cinnamon incense;
The carnivorous chill soaks through layers of clothing
Damp is joined to forlorn anticipation
That the storm will pull a black curtain
Across the streaks of sunset
Eliminating light.

2.
Eerie rays of light from the lighthouse
Perched on boulders in an angry ocean
Emit ghostly fog through a macramé of lace tree tops
As dawn pervades a pine forest
Where a boy is lost
His furtive calls muffled
By a carpet of autumn needles, fractured twigs
And draped low hung boughs.
In the distance he hears the speed of cars
On a highway up ahead.

3.
Pole streaked snow
A thousand lines downhill
A skier's view of a nestled town
At the foot of heaven's shadows
Snow carpeted mountains
Where a road winds

Through pinnacles
And gains its vistas, overlooks
And visions of a downhill racer
Careening and soaring to the vast wilderness
Of empty skies.

4.

The shouting whistle of the midnight train in the distance
The jostling yellow light of a sultry wind
A garnet ghost rushing closer
Trees sway on the riverbank
The Chicago-Huron line joined by sparks alight on the rail;
Across Lake Superior ice and snow float;
Tumble from the berth inside our boxcar
Sheets unmade, bathroom door ajar
Flight of lust not far behind.

5.

Chips of falling light dazzle
Like a tourmaline cartwheel,
A thin crimson glass pane
Paints three stories of a Montreal library
Where stands a street lamp.
One shudders as the falling chips abound
In salmon tints and melt;
The air fills anew with crystals
Which fall and fall again
Piling up the snow embankment
In swirling revelations
In an escarpment of darkly crimson stone.

6.
The black pawed calico cat sits
Disdainfully eyeing the shallow pond of golden coye;
Lemon trees line against the high fence
Fragrance lingers.
The blue door to the yard opens
A young toddler in grey overalls
And red cap over silver blond curls
Runs amuck crushing the squash trumpets
Knows enough to skirt his mother's poppies
And gleefully gives the calico a firm smack.

7.
an older white man with fuzzy short brown hair
in a green and black plaid shirt and a purple and tan
paisley pants
looks to be a caricature of Eugene Kelly
singing in the rain
whirling around a park tether pole
with a trowel for a garden dig in his ring-finger hand
his lithe body bent to behold
a branch of budding willow
he plants as he hums
by autumn the branch will be a sapling.

Salt Lake City Going Home

Passionate orange soil littered by flecks of metallic gold
Murky fog misted puddles
Protruding slats of orange rock, fir and chaparral
Bright green moss adheres on dark grey brittle branches
In the port there's a neighborhood of trees.
Up high where the elevation is five thousand feet
Snow suds drip off the pines
Ice crystallized water spikes flow from the flumes;
The silver track lantern light on a telephone pole is blinking
As the train proceeds along the track
Beneath bare branches that shake free of a burden of snow
The dark ground covered by Styrofoam
Cottony puffs are falling
From tree tops in a blizzard wind
Fresh poured marshmallow
Soaks the street
Where a partially fallen cross hangs in the balance;
The Southern Pacific TTK train
Passes white candlestick pines
The door of a cab box house of one room stands open
Onto the summit field on the ridge
Rainbow at west end of valley
Mists hang over the twisting all granite valley;
Twice I retrace my return to my seat
Through the dining car
Translucent ice at Yuma Dam at nine thousand feet
Silver dark blue brush strokes accentuate
The stress of traveling for photography
It's been upsetting – China peaks thick with snow
And wooden timber peering through clouds
Into a stark blue sky
Far below a red cab carrying a vivid orange truck

Emerges in this lonely austere passage
Tell me you have not discarded the honesty of life
Ghosted flock of forlorn branches on frozen ponds
Blue moon over snow banks
River of Donner Lake indigo cold
Bare tusks of scraggy branches
Two black roads through a grey shrouded forest
A black car barely escapes notice.
There's thirty-five feet of snowfall at this 6,984 feet elevation
Light snows toss about
Leaning poles, a camaraderie of pressure to relent
The state is dominated by an industry of solar panels
A descent through four minutes of darkness
On the route to Truckee
Flash light for a photographic second
Winter is much better than summer
Lead grey inky lake despite blue charcoal sky
Reflects an abundance of trees, bluish center
Patina at water's edge, insensate, colorless
Snow skeleton on flat branch
A balancing rod, keel of thin whiskers
Despairing arms
Dark grey creeks like old roads
Slink below a preponderance of snow
And icy platelets where water collects
Beneath an HIV pattern of ice-breaking skin
A shadow frost painted coagulation
East Truckee is a lane
Through a Nevada desert of cement asbestos
Very grainy white snow tent tops on a continuation of
    mountains.
An avalanche of rocks held in place on a slope
Tufts of green algae-like brush
Crimson grass, a slant of light purple flowers
Sequeled by a passive reluctance to venture further

Truckee Meadows, a canyon of flumes
House cabins crowded into rows along a river
Tin roofs, wooden verandas, two rocking chairs
A moment of lake, a blue blue windy plain.
Such a contrast to the soft blue velvet staircase
Of the Salt Palace in downtown Salt Lake City
The new City Creek of orange brick, white jade, rust,
Yellow, aqua glass, horseshoe walk, all this beauty –
Isolated traffic.
Across the street sits the Joseph Smith Memorial Square
The black dome and nighttime light of the State Capitol
    Plaza
Behind it against a placid sky the Wasatch Mountains
The Reagan Primary in Jacksonville Florida
Is hosting the countdown between Romney and Gingrich
There's anger on Capitol Hill for the true conservative
Arizona Governor wants secure borders.
Medical chat in the car at snow-deep summit
A man sipping red wine says he's been living in a dream
A couple plays dice, he's still working on a vodka lime
As the California Zephyr slips through the silence
The Truckee River is black like in a black and white photo
Along a snow encrusted bank where rock face peers from
    snow
Pines are wedged in splintered rock
Slats inside the train tunnel flicker with jasper and snow.

At Soda Springs Valley on the return home a week later
On the #5 Zephyr
The kids are boasting about jazz and forty-niners
That's all there is unless you stay home to watch re-runs
At Yuba Gap in 1952 a snow slide buried a train
And the Army, Navy, Pacific Telephone and Telegraph
and Lake Spaulding
Dug travelers out of the snow over three days.

In the observation car sunlight spills
Over a hill like a glowing orb
In the café lounge, it's diet coke, chips, a hot dog;
The bartender talks about his mother who's ninety
She gets out, she's doing something, stays active,
We're in Blue Canyon at Dutch Flat and Gold Run
I hiked Zion one summer while I was still married
We climbed the rock face above the waterfalls
The moment I knew we were leaving
I called my mother.
Sun causes the forest to fade
My brother will drive in to eat
Indian curry and syrup pudding with me
When I attend my next class on attachment
I began lunch with a crimson vodka tonic
A Cape Cod cosmopolitan diet and Ceasar
The mud is churned up by the rain
It's dark brown slaked by rust dirt
Colfax has A-line roofs and three story inset gables
I can still feel the chill from the platform
At Truckee when I took in the fresh air.

Cachet

An incurable romantic observes wind blown pink cachet
Hundreds of falling cherry blossom petals
Swirling in a tempest like new butterflies
The fierce tan bud-backed carnation alights
Like pre-ripe small inedible berries
Moss chartreuse baize sprung branches
With elfin aggrieved thistle
A drunken carousel of spinning streamers
Of May Day hawthorn tassels
That wind up the pole in brown, crimson and carnelian
Exalted hymns of dance weaving a pinwheel
Oh! What a windy spring morn
Spirited flurries of flying ecstasy
A pity of whirling blossoms

A quizzical repression
Reciprocal
Overwhelm, overpower, crush, subdue
Itinerant, traveler, drifter, loner
The pale lime paint is barely dry
An essential part bringing forth fruition
Fertile pollination in the enchanted meadow
A chaste, pure, wondrous inspiration regenerates
The dilemma of beauty, of nature at its infinitesimal seed
Its clairvoyant wanderings attuned to none other than
    absolute form
Its private awakenings, melodious populations, cultivations
Languid beneficent marvels, constant realizations
Endemic fertilizations: a mathematics of dispersed
    scatterings
Like magical stars kissing the tips of brilliant crimson
    flowers

Winter Song

What one hears,
But sees rock with icy frozen stream gusher
Arrested floes like granite stalks
Surface of big Klamath Lake striated by ice cracks
Glacial mud stirring like a stymied sludge of river
Rust lightened wheat mats emerge flattened

In an inlet beneath a frozen pond
Shadows of glittery ice hammers, algae green moss
A quiet muffled silence glides over pocked snow
Through the dark tunnel windows of forest line appear
Snapshots of gushing granite as we approach the summit
Pocked snow lines crevices where no one has ever walked

Crystalline roots dangle in a dormant hush
Frozen stone water a seasonal image
He's gone for a walk in the rain
She's stayed home in front of the hearth

It's rained all night; the fresh smell of rain comes
through the window
Thick black clouds with mist hover as low as the swollen
    river
At two it's a drive into town to the library and art gallery
The dog like an autistic child fawns for chronic attention
Jalapeno-ginger jam on blueberry scones
Walking on stilts a student is two stories tall

Petals in the tea, a mixture of rose and orange pekoe
All flowers conjure up memories as if secrets drift on wind
Fried garlic shrimp and gin for midnight sun on snow tundra
A sachet of chicalote brings dawn through the window

All colors of a prism spill across the covers
Delight, its own window, opens where bright sun breaks
   through

Winter Equinox

Like a single line of shining light
Winter's dark elliptical equinox
Extends or contracts
Depending upon the hilarious
Breaking glass of ice
Pitched by bolts of crossed
Blizzards raging over
Frozen floods
Of conical tunnels.

At its ecliptic
When dawn measures dusk
Black gold petroleum
Splashes to sea
Like a spigot forgot
Ruining shallow black land
Building up excrescences on low branches
Of sticky plum and cherry waste
Blood sausage in appearance
As any black husk raspberry.

Black tributaries run silent
Through the epiphanies
Of deepest dark
In daylight they sit
Protruding spines of harbors
Like a suppression
A line of spars surrounding an oil spill
Sloshing it like cargo onto the land.

Centerpiece

A brown sugar bowl
With floating jasmine soft
White flower

A pleasing motive
For a glimpse of joy

Oddly it's the garish twang
Of grey blue, crimson orange,
Dizzy lemon green and a blur
Of ebony fast cars in the alley
That baffle
The senses.

A Feast of Apples

A feast of tiny apples
Bobs in the water-filled barrel
On the yard patio
For days until pulped
A thrill of puce
Conceited and imposing prosperity
The plum that sits at the bottom
Kills with overindulgence
A handsome Cognac, leek or clove of garlic
Clash of class with artifice
Subliminal bondage, tensile impertinence
Divine immunity, heady jigger,
A torrential quickly wasting weed
Filling the sop-run
To the knees, possibly wetting the hem
With an inundation of salty corn.
Plops of rain convey
A tedium that invalidates tolerance
Like a birdbath on the lawn
A glissando at gloaming.
Through midnight when the slaked barrel
Floats the hundred or so apples
In pure rainwater with the night sky
As still as a crescent sliver of silver moon
A bird splashes, rouge apples on the surface
Are their own tranquility.

Train from Quebec City to Nova Scotia

The beach late afternoon is untouched,
Pristine in crystalline clarity,
Gentler waves than choppy Atlantic murky blue,
Night twinkles over the land
Which hosts ash forests on all isles?
In port villages peaceful and possibly unknowable
Except for the train
A solitary trodden path sneaking above
The darkest plateaus in the strait
That knows only years of snowfall and canoe.
Stone houses, elegant in a promise
Of early day quiet reveal the barest of desires,
People have drifted here
From the punctuality of cities,
A brief rectitude as they rise
In plumed cages, blocks behind
The Biblioteque Nacionale.
Men in trousers bare chested
Stride through grass waist high
To the red mud creek two feet down,
They rent a home with veranda
In a cove on the Laurent strait.
Cornfields raked, earth in need of fertilization,
Most crop will go to feed;
To this it is said
One has been a father often,
I slept on the train which was late into Czerny,
The St. Laurent quiet as a jewel.
I have waited winter to shut myself
In against the outside world

Inside a studio in a brick warehouse
On the waterfront wharf,
The flappers in the kitchen covering the balcony door
Snappy in the cross wind
Sounding much like a man cracking his knuckles;
Laughter like coin money spilling
Over the rail from a top floor balcony,
Joyous, sparkling with gaiety,
Spontaneously fresh and well-acquainted,
Not yet intimate, a picture of cascading
Snow and ice breaking up over Jasper Falls,
A brevity of conversation
Where from wee morning hours a prism
Of light glitters with glints
Of spar and stream and falling ice –
I always see an art gallery
If I'm going to stay
Somewhere longer than a week.
Nine blocks – Terminal, South, Morris
Bishop, Spring Garden, Salter, Blowers,
Sackville, at Prince there is no signal,
Each city by taxi, tourist spots, restaurants, fortress
All the way out on the Sound
Parking garages, cafes with yellow deco vase
Lights, Marriott's Spirit Café, echoes a dream
Where I can't find the car, anxiety shows in deep
Sunk dark grey eyes, dark puffy shadows below
The eyes, creases at the thin nose and thinner lips,
Blond hair dying to its roots, swam first thing
Every morning before seven
Ate a buffet ham, red bell pepper, cheddar omelet
Walked to the park on the water
Where ash grows like lean-to's in a fence line
From their own bereft wood
As it lies submerged to some powerful

Anchor of root beneath rainwater,
Elephantine-cut birch like pipes
Or horn blowers emerge from sandy earth
Flooding through a forest of ash
Reflects the bark of wood and sky,
Where the light falls onto leaves
Below timberline the soil appears
Like strata as the train hurries
From Campbellton over the Laon Bridge
The first smoking stop after Moncton.

Blowing Glass at the Harbor

Windy roads to gravel beach
Remind me a bit of Inverness
The strait is so calm the fish jump
Can be seen a quarter of a mile across,
Grey stone tower above a softwood forest
The Metchek home has sandstone pillars
He owns four hotels in Halifax but not
Dalhousie University which has eleven blocks
Old buildings, social science, art, Inglis Street
Rows of heritage houses, stone two story each,
Public gardens given Victoria by her father Edward
Spring Street shops are the most trendy
George Street has the city museum and gallery,
At the water the ferry comes in from Dartmouth to casino
That sits at the end of skyway next to dockyards with
    small ships
Old hotels, Radisson on Hollis,
Uptown has the Marriott Courtyard
Yellow frosted glass, 7-story with courtyard café
A limo takes me down the coast
Three hours past Peggy's Cove to the resorts,
It's not hurricane season
Although lights are doused due to power outage,
Candles in the bar where I have a window seat
White cottage houses on every hillside face the choppy
    ocean
I unwind with a Vermouth and Caesar salad,
Indian curry will have to wait
As will the ten o'clock invitation
From the very tall bony man smoking a reefer
Who listens to Gloria Patri
While he blows glass through a long metal rod

It bubbles dark red
Dominates forest green
Then extends as though he is playing the sax
Bright sparks giving off emotive rebounds,
By ten when the limo lets me off
Mist has descended so low to the water
One can't see the street.

What Is Known

Futilitarian moldy dampness
Poland's cynicism
Garish future man as gas pump
Bombs falling in Poland Street Warsaw
Alicja Halicka cubist still life
A hard female in a bar
Glass of burgundy wine
Purple red, life like blood
Tamara de Lempika's calla lilies a shade grey-bluer
Than Frida Kaehlo all slanted Rivera colors
Art Beyond Borders, Awdziejcsyk
Red, pink, brown metallic ceramic on paper
Kuczynski stretch limo parked across a divide
Girl in leotard skirt on wire
Delicate balancing act,
Jean-Louis Foran's strong imprint of enduring skill
William Strang's Scottish girl flowing red hair
Beige crème blouse the look of absence of softness
Portrait of James McNeil nightmarish dead
Arc d'tromphe lit up portal to Wodiczko in dark night
A grab bag from which choice is taken without advance
Miroslav Balka on exhibit at the Tate
Wood box installations
Perspectives on steel, how it is,
What is known.

Leaving at Night

Fickle mooring
To pull away soundlessly
Leaving the coast without its dock;
Persuasive departure
Fishing pole still attached
To its mule,
Subtropical cyclone diminishes
Even the city lights flicker

San Juan fortress on the ocean
Declares graveyards, crypts, crosses
While far out beneath moon on tin
Ocean liners like narrow streets
Move about relentlessly like high sea walls
Covered by sea urchins by the time waves
Roll in planks of wood,
Wrought iron horses turned prophets
From where the storm released an embankment

50 Pesos

The damage is done
He's fallen cord rising
Against the rippling wind
From a Blackhawk helicopter
With Border Disrupt Teams
As we advance on land with low trees
Easily fifty smugglers in black nylon
Fighting river tide beneath low brush
In a motel below the border
Jimi Hendrix and Sunset Park
Can be heard in dying gasps
Out on the street.

In the Field of Rustling Grasses

Against the only boundary
A faded gray wooden bucket
Rests below a rust copper fence

Chimes in a window
Cantilevered open
Twinkle in a brief wind
As the moving wind
Collects
Over the wispy tips of grass
Waist high

I've stood like this
A checkered white and blue wool shawl
Wrapped about my shoulders
Many a morning
Waiting for inspiration
While inside the two room cottage house
The others begin to stir.

From a Stand of Walnut Trees

The sun's shadow stretches
Over an abundance of cupped-waif poppies
The overbearing prickly reddish light purple
Beard stemmed cacti shaving the height of delicate lilies,
A tarnished bronze bracelet with thin crimson ribbon
Lies over the parchment page
Of poetry written by Walt Whitman
In a yard populated by roses trumpeting in action
For the sly wind coming up through the vale.
In her garden overgrown with flowers
There are hydrangea, orange dahlias, marigolds, snap peas,
Tea roses without a smell, epistle wands, herbs, violet
    and yellow,
Spinach salad diced with walnuts, currants and red grapes,
Humus buttered flat bread lightly toasted and mint tea,
Crumpets and marmalade-brushed scones
And two stanzas each of love verse slipped through a ring.

Aptos, California

Walk on the Santa Cruz beach
Color of sand grainy gold what I'm used to seeing
Waves at 7pm wash over the sand bar like vanishing sand
Which by 9pm sky gray blue to water reflects like ice
Along entire sand ocean pool having risen to full tide
A surmise of watery depth
Without visible grains of darkness filling the pond.
Young skinny preteens crowd the sand,
Aging white haired man and wife fly a kite,
Girls skip over cement stairs
Even though low wall is boarded up at entrances,
The high pier with glass lounge at end
And row of pink, blue, green houses along lone road
    down to beach.
Otherwise outdoor café with bandstand fills up by
    sundown
And the waitresses resemble beautiful coiffed blondes in
    tight tights,
Poems like shimmering haze saturate
A group of thirty avidly listens inside the coffee shop.
A child clapping his hands isn't yet mindful
Of the sandcastle that sits
At the edge of sand crumbling toward the delta.
Intense conversation between friends walks no lines,
No disagreement over the tip for dinner
No thought has a couple taking digital photos of the
    mesmerizing ocean
While a curious seagull picks at pizza lying in an open box,
We do not consider for long the fact that caffeinated tea
Cannot be drunk at night before bed.
This is normal – a relaxing ease watching the tide come in.
That's as good as it gets.

Two surfers paddle while standing –
Both are sturdy as windsurfers without sails.
Lethargy of divorce still sticks
Like an inability to be free to do as one likes.
Light rain in the street light and damp pavement
Makes for a quiet restoration long sought for.
An incessant drip outside the window
Leaves no permanent stain to trace by morning.

Recollections of Arabstar and Mir

False starts come and go
With the day's lack of inspiration
I wonder, will there be a breeze
Shall I dream of a sandy beach and cool blue ocean?
Of waves pounding the harbor wall all night
Hurling strands of sea weed, tubes and pebbles
Along a coastline strewn with dunes;
The air condition as a slow hum
Sounds like the music score of 2001
A shark image-enhancer space station that looms
In outer space grinding away
A giant motor taking pictures shore to shore
A hundred a minute, steel mirror plates
Revolving in darkness where not a storm
Or dawn penetrates;
Like some promised messiah hypnotic Merlin
Civilization is to military science
A thousand labyrinths tugging at the green seas
Beneath myriads of droplets of blue skies
Blood as inconsequential as Jason Pollock
Casting spells on maze walls concrete and mirror;
Oh! Couldn't we take the kids to see the clown?
The mocking fakir who dies in battle,
Ambiguous sweetness of casks of cassava
Ecology listening secretly to private intimacies
The ocean out flowing from the land
That answers its purpose boundlessly, eternally,
Ceaselessly as a petition of science
For the configuration of industrial machines
Overworked as derelict ebony scrawny wolves;

Native land, fatherland of listless vigor
Into what state of being will we gradually pass?
Shall we go to an omission of fact?
Shall we warble with a dialect towards the land?
Viviparous living below the troposphere
Shows like transitory translations
That are easily understood and unmistakable.

Plain on the Moon's Surface

The puckered astringent lime taste on the salt rim
For the old girls who bump-ass the jitterbug to the Jamaica
Come to place love letters in stone walls of fences
    running far to field
Pushing a barrow for a highballing highbinder –
This is Henry Miller's new asceticism on agglutinin
Lazy naked females reclining on velvet couches
The age of reason nothing compared to an age of consent
Jack Lord the young John Kennedy the aglet pinned
As tidy a drawing room cord to call up the manservant
To treat the ague with the medicine for chills and fevers
An aikido of nonresistance of using another man's hate
    against him
As filching a spot not frozen over in ice to shunt the
    sewer waste into;
I remember William Attwood whose disheartened lack
    of enthusiasm
Made schools of slack bobbies whose founder of police
Sir Robert Peel
But for a mean tide washed in too early in Kipling's
    collapse of a circus tent
Proved little better than Rose Feld's opinion that life
    didn't live up to its rancor anyhow
As pointed the old brass and Gus Russo calling in the
    sword such as it is
Cocktail appetizer and soda biscuit at three a wealthy
    man's champagne of ease
J.T. Farrell's removal of all deficiencies confirmed the
    education was a success
Despite the fact that Kennedy's football ran out the clock
And Dr. Dorothy Otnow Lewis' probes of a sadistic killer
Are coffee-table book references by Robin O'Neill the

> weekend chef
> Wherein we all worry on occasion the ocean unfurls
>   with enough abalone
> Much less that hypochondriacs drink absinthe prior to
>   recollecting the war.

Horizon

Faith like brightness seen from afar
After a term of obligation
Becomes a panicle of pantheism
Kiss of peace
By which all endeavors are tried;
I will have been forsaken as empty chatter
To lose so much as a smile
For what good is an erasure
When depression reads like something broken
Each line a dislocation
Reticence
A despondent remnant
Of an escarped surface or crater
Into which snow stores up inside
In quantities of wind-driven piled drifts

At the tide pool bottom
Rock fashioned by repetitive waves
For as long as wearisome hard worked middle years
Glint like blue and green gemstones
In a swirl of compromise
Where transparent flecks float to the surface
Transitory laughter in lilting humor
Rises in cadence through the open window
Of a white painted country cottage
That sits without a fence on the bluff.
I don't have the heart
To board the place up to leave
The instep of your promising sea.

Delirious in your jasmine
Of red littered seaweed over sand bars

Frequent tides of passion shipwrecked
I sometimes awaken in deep regret
The damp of a drenching rain
Having produced a great longing
To stray into your farthest
Westward diurnal sunsets
Every horizon vouched for
Until I know you to clasp the sail
And hold the wind
And make me cry

I hesitate to call upon you
As freely as I think I'd like
When you leave me
I purchased your type of bed
So that when I sleep alone
It is as though you are still here.

Quick Turns

A series of quick turns
Of a ballerina twirling across the stage
A pink satin bodice and pink chiffon short skirt
A pink net over her points-gathered bun
The train passes through wide open spaces
Along scattered ponds, the new Antioch toll
Two brick factories, Riverview Lodge & Bar
At Antioch Marina, squares of new houses
Martinez has new county records building
Across from the new station of brick, blue glass
The question of how to keep the moment more present
It flees too fast, clients in San Ramon, Benicia and Lake
 County
Evaluations for children, can they draw a house, pick out
A doll, a soldier, their mother the protector, their father
 the wise
I know many people although I find it hard to engage
As though it is I watching myself with raised arms and
 pointed toe
It's been hours since dress rehearsal since we bowed
White gladiolas like small doves come to rest nestled in
 our arms
We are a group of therapists for teen prisoners
No patient exists without bars;
They are snagged by mental and jacket buckle restraints
Paths they turned down at fifteen robbing liquor stores,
 hotwiring cars
When they were hot with anxious rebellion
A dad out nights to see a mistress
Their mum dead beat tired looking after two babies
Certain they had good friends and would stay young forever.
She twirls faster and faster her pink chiffon an almost blur

From head to toe absolutely controlled
A streak or striation
In the mirror there are fifty images.
From the opera matinee wearing shirt tails
A second cup for mocha latte and fag
Across from du film where the girls are rehearsing
For a performance at the Alexandre Gaudet Ltd.
   Warehouse stage
Aboard the de la Gare-Mont train putting out of Toronto
Where after dark, deep water reflects trees ancient and
   tagged
As a hybrid of pines or birch – all tangled with the moon.
While we are on the road the company pays
A suite, private shower, hall, dormer windows
Green raised carpet, classical music, marble bath
Tea and whiskey at four, English muffin at nine in the
   morning
We gather like perfumed old bugs tired of strolling
Across from an avenue of old English storefronts
At the Government plaza on the green in front of old
   stone buildings
With worn copper turrets and stained red and yellow
   glass windows,
The taxi departs at ten, crammed full with foreigners
Taking us across the Saint Laurent up the coast
To the Protestant steeple church train station
Where we wait the midnight train to the Great Lakes
Its gleaming yellow light shining on us
Dimming the view our cameras can take.
I've yearned for a long walk up Rue Ursalines
To see the new churches and open air markets
To pass through the tunnel to parliament
Its black statues lingering on the white tile
Jazz speak easy and perdition apricot aged brandy,
But it's ten at night before dinner is served on the Lorne

Salad and anchovy, tossed egg, tri-tip, meringue sherbet
Talk on the town an Air France plane disappears over Brazil,
We too are content in Canadian fields of the ice
Full bar pate, bouillabaisse, strudel and always
    overflowing Merlot;
Breakfast is steak and Vermouth, for me no cost
Because I arrive late; I tip a five anyway to show my
    gratitude.

Haute Couture

Females in teal masks
Descend stairs of ebony carpet
Over pristine marble
Their lithe languorous bodies
Sheathed in backless flowing opera pink
And vivid tangerine silk gowns,
With four inch steel spike heels of midnight blue
Driven by ambition and cost
Cocaine breathless wonder
Chartreuse chopsticks
Spearing golden beehives
Haute couture
Making its grand entrance
On a hazy summer eve
Chandeliers blazing in wall sized mirrors
Like twinkling ice.

 Light and shade
College age men dressed all in black with white ties
Dance cartwheels
Beautiful females in white trousers and white brassieres
With black gloves twirl
Together the men like intermissions
Where the couples dance tango
Black holds white like a weeping willow
Sweeping the stage of regret
The lights turn blue
The men become shadow-like
Their counterparts like swans.

Russian Ships on the Sea

Distinctive green wine bottles like actual glass
Mixed with dark brownish black
On a table of a ship in a battle night
Alexandra Yakusheva commits pessimism with wine
Poor injured young soldier left to die in the snow
Plum and red etchings of pine trees in the corner
It is the mind to be a hearty drinker and an intellectual
Sipping one's purple burgundy at the bar counter
Behind the green curtain of the billiard room
The psychology of practiced detachment for the clinic
With so much military death
Evacuated into Savrosov's city churches of the wine pond,
There is no way to replenish coats or boots or its youth
When the wine pond is the sole warmth
Nicholas II stands proud his uniform grey blue as the
    eventual sky
Color precise, conscious detail, depictions of life
The indefatigable winters of 1812
Baksheev family of three at dinner
Situated around the dinner table surrounded by bookshelves
Is The Prose of Life of Germany
Girl in chiffon black and white, golden hair pulled back
Fascinated by her reflection
Seated on a rock in a pond painted grey, black and brown,
Two young men in long swimsuits of basic red brown
    like coveralls
Stretched out on a rocky beach are officers on a day off
The certain knowledge the world of the portrait
Represented by a youthful young brunette in pink collar
Like Jolita Kelias' woman seated in her living room
A bowl for long stem yellow, pink and tan gladiolas
A welcome cheery exuberance of confidence;
Still, the pond as depiction of Mashinka's upside down empire
Is coming of age in a height of promise.

Two in the Morning, Ryer's Island

A translucent aquamarine blue glass bowl
Catches the light of snowfall
From the dining room chandelier
A navel orange
Gravenstein apple
Bartlett pear
Callifornia state fair grown
Seedless wine red grapes
And five icy black-purple figs
Boast of orchards in the flooded
Delta near the Sacramento River.
An aluminum ladder in spring
Stands below a tree of limes
Over the tops tangerine trees
Can be seen in abundance
To the distant sky
The picker's wristwatch forgotten
Inside the cloth bag that hangs
From a red fence.
The chef at the breakfast inn
With ten tables is an import
From the French Quarter in New Orleans
A black sassy obese homosexual
Who wears a shower cap
And slings fried eggs, yam slices and hash.
He lives with his old lady in a small flat
Beneath a dizzy winking dance parlor
Where the four story stone cement
Is rifled with ivy vines.
The jury is out
Having deliberated on the stabbing murder

Of a victim tossed from a black van
At two in the morning onto a street corner
Near the Ryer's Island gasoline store
Closed every Sunday.

Spring

Gophers out everywhere today
The dog corners one to a hole
Barks.

Too brief a breeze gives relief
A boy with a kite chases
His shadow.

Early spring
Olive quince shrubs, citron bell-shaped flowers
Forsythia.

The fox runs with hounds yelping
Henna, rufous, a quick blur
The hare hunt.

Summer

Afternoon threadbare gusty halls
Through branches a glimpse
The madder lake.

Mackerel blue evening
Muggy heat suspends wind
Harbor boats line the gas pump.

Smothering aggravation
Canvassing for signatures
Leaves me tired.

Jaundiced skin
An old woman lies bedridden
Flies have minds of their own.

The soil of blackberries
Raked free of vines
Holds repressed fragrance.

Languorous heat, manly desire
Saxophone angst
The new moon lingers.

I know summer not at all
Image escapes me until a draught
Fans.

Shells like ridged half moons
Dollars with stars
A bottle of smooth scarlet glass.

Stains like Braille
A cantaloupe spills seeds
Conjectures, sleeping dogs lie.

Whispers
Lemonade streaks on a pitcher
A tempest gathers brisk gusts.

Even without mild occurrence
The deers make haste
In a flurry.

A glimpse of moors
Only a cabin alight
Redundancies of the heart.

Countless deers
More than a crowded forest
At daybreak not a one found.

Hunt and peck
31 words a minute
the price of tea for twenty.
One dog, ten sheep
They amble steadily
Pushing against the windy lough.
So it goes, a bramble with thorns
The weight of branches
Pulling raked words.
Haiku, haiku –
Mist, a sliver of moon, frost
Icicles, points.
Snowy owl, snowfall
An egret snagged, flight
Precarious, wing torn.

The walk to Stonehenge
Through a tunnel, up an incline
Mythical circle,
We converse, students
Druid stones impossibly placed
Shadows listening.
Archetypal rock –
We're each from different countries
Like old folk.

Willows like falling tears
Drench the ground piteously –
Oh, the mood clings.
Lives wait unreasonably
Chill freezes
The heavens part with a storm.
Memories also
Linger in advance,
Children in a playground laugh.
How many bridges must one cross?
River or field,
endless acres.

A jade jar
Collects with pennies –
Fifty for milk and a caramel square.
Rubber ducks line a window sill
They darken
Until they are seen from outside,

Hornblowers
The trees shake free –
Figs like squashed gloves fall in a bronze rain.
Leaves ensconced with spines and mottled gauze
Cradle in a cantering wind.

She awakens to a breeze
Pressing between floorboards,
His arm draws her,
So much commotion
Plates rattle – breakfast at eight
Kids leave for school fast.
Aria, octave, soprano
She practices
Higher and higher.

Dunes at first light
Azure waters stretching like tin –
Scintillating sun.
Tarnished blue boats with oars
Moored on sand, August
Races to the point – heat wave.
I grew up on Albany bay
Oil slicks like dark red seaweed
Hundreds of white sails
At summer's end like kites,
The water serene
The orange bridge glinting, a horizon
separating sea and sky.
Our house was one of twelve
The hill forested, by night
A light on the pier, prisoner's island, ships.
Today at sixty my home sits far
Through the Richmond tunnel in acres of pennyroil
Afternoon tea sees a man fishing
Off a boat.

In the massacre of
Spindly aspen, leafless totems
Tractor clearings;
Terns no longer nest

They fly asleep for months –
Only stealth hawks hover.
Climates advance on wings.
Sliding avalanches coffin
Ice takes root;
Deer migrations, a thousand hoofs at once
Clopping stampedes
Heard long in the night,
Antler remnants –
Tracks through the snow
Wild branches.

Winter

I spent a summer on ice
Cliffs drifted off
calving ice ominous
As gunshot
The only sound for miles,
At night ice cracks too softly,
A caribou can fall off a shelf
A lad trains himself
By climbing
Through a sky window,
Precarious balance can kill

Saplings on ice
Form a regiment –
Sprouts in every direction.

At the end of life
One packs in for a long winter,
Without need of spending.

Regrets have their own distance
Children their own leafy arbors
      A wind storm.

Cool as chilling ice
A sliver of moonlight wanes.
Darkness, harsh pulse
The wind rattles the shutters.
A downpour of rain
Ice drips on the pane,
      The blue lamp is on, misty.

Snow penetrates
Divorce is imminent,
> He argues non stop all night.
A continual signal –
The ship at sea
The port is out of reach.

A lone piercing light
A call picks apart the dark
Steady as she blows.

 Boredom creates a rift
> The dog chases his tail
> A man sips tea.
Low arousal –
> She's home too often
> She complains of his messy clothes.
Dog wades into the ocean for the stick
> He is gone an hour:
> She thinks.

She was in love once
> It was like magic
> Overly connected; loved.

Lightning flickers, black clouds gloam,
A transient cold front,
Drenched rain deafens.

A cacophony drowns out
Scarcely audible sound
Muffled cries, silent.

Sleet! A short man hurries,
A newspaper for a hat,

   Cursing at cats.
He buys a green umbrella
Slow pace to the firm
   Ice litters the street.
Reports on his desk pile up
Bleak sky, snow storm
   Indifference, a skill.
Lightning cracks vibrant pink
Rushing water pours
Gutters fill instantly.

You think loudly
As though thinking soothes irritation.
   Doors fly open.
Wind snowdrifts
A grey fox holds a cariole in its teeth,
Wings flutter.

Unpunctual middle-age
The silver resonates brass
At dinner.
Manure churned mud
Sparse sentimentality
Small hours gut sting.
An adopted transference
Shame
Their verve acts violative of norms.

Corn cake
Melting butter and strawberry jam
The knife makes a clean slice.
Still life –
Iced persimmon, sliced fig, guava
To the artist honest means.
Bare branches with a single leaf –

Despite a fierce wind
Life remains fast.

Black maroon lake, a reflection
Storm in turbulence,
Always hail falls.

Imprints

Deciduous sloughing off
Like a snake shedding skin
The first sign of menopause
Hunger a persistant obsession
Making love, a strong desire despite the ravages.
Routines become hard to tolerate
A trip across the state seems a good answer,
Everything from the drawers into the back of the van
Alone, the long highway is its own purpose.
Only the mind wanders,
Absence a complete distraction
The van bed, a hardness good for the soul.

In days when I was working my thesis
All ideas were a variegation of promise
Youth a sap collecting sugar
A perpetual plentitude for all attractions
An afternoon with a husband
Watching spindles of rain collect
The image on the wall a bluish imprint
The air sultry and damp,
Humid heat its own compensation
Arduous love bent like a flexible bow.
Of course the body has its persuasions
It tires in due course of languid momentum
Frees itself between rhythms
Longs for the past or inserts into the present,
One year I stayed gone a semester
The grand tetons pillared tall above mountain lakes
The lowest point grew emerald hibiscus
I spent the drenching rain inside a tent
The worst of the day brushing for arrowheads.

I knew a man who junked his camper
After spending two years in Isolation Wilderness.

Let's not tell ourselves it's all for knowledge
This wavering between idiom and image
The language of the heart
A seeking of the very resonance it wants to be.
The idea of image as a connection
The likeness between mother and child –
Imprints take with lovers also.
I dreamed Lazarus climbed down from his ladder
Took the ladder into the house
And set it against a window.
Once revived, we return.

El Escritorio

1.

No le dijo que tu me gusta mas
Que todo el mundo es mucho alto
Cual las estrellas o las mesas,
Tanto par ver es echarme de menos.
No le dijo la cortesia tener la intencion
De estoy despierto o pensare
A mendo en tu
Tu ultimo hace prometer
Y espere que tu confesare.
Hace muchas tiempo
Estar contento de a menudo
En desearle un profundo
Quiere decirle que tu esta cados.
Lo peor es estoy muy agradecido,
Sin duda alguna me gusto los dulces
Diga me la verdad que estoy
Aprovechar el momento de traer el paraguas
Para tener que confesarle muchas sinceras.
Me aparece bueno
Tendre todos noches
Acaba de dormir
Repita debiles con su permiso.

2.

Entonces nadie terminar
De veras la filete picante
La cereza esta el cordero parecerse

Me aconseja sobre las papayas,
Entonces de prisa recorder
Alguien que trabajar despacio
Para postre
No hace nadie
Quedarse al sol sin pidiendolo.
La criada esta bastante
De prisas a menudo llueve.
El recuerdo es el rio,
El asiento del estrella lloria lavar
Me gusta mas para digame
Cuando tu tendere nadie.
Advisarme.

3.

Cada vez llego a tu estar cansado
Cuando llamarse por subterraneo
Cuando el ojo dormirse
Me encuentro tu domingos
Se sienten en fila
Se tiene razon

Siempre reina las amor.
Cuando deseando
Estoy esperando
Hace nunca mas
No me preocupe
Donde es posible para calcular
Las distancias a tus cantaros.

4.

Tu estara sorpendido de saber
He cogido un poco en amar,
Tu repuesta es atento
Querido amor no me falta nada
Conteste que esta muy equivocado
Porque no tenia problamente
Pasada nunca.
Domina los restos
Le alegria.

5.

No deseo mucho
Son importantes, cerca del escritorio
Emociantes, debir decider
Magnifico estar en camino
La luna es gustar
Pero los demas esta despertarse
El ano que viene de antano
La bondad en la alma brisa
Aprisa citar encima del vale
Quiero si siguente lo que arregular
Los animos obtener la manana,
Explicar la comedia
O anunciar cualquier grito del reconocer.
Casi llegando en la tarde
El amor llega siempre por tren.

I don't ask for much
Very important nearest the writing practice
Emotions, one must decide

Magnificent to be on one's personal path
The moon is for pleasure
But the rest for awakening
Kindness the airy sojourn of love
Swiftly to arrive at an appointment near one's worth
I want yes to follow that which has arranged
The soul of the next morning
To explain the comedy of life
Or to present whichever shout of intuition.
Almost arriving in the afternoon
Love arrives only on the train.

6.

La gana irse
Se escucha indigena –
El descendiente se hace felicitar
Los estudiantes durante del descanso
La funcion de la baile se empiezan
Guapo, dulce, pronunciado en la fila
En el desfile estan emociantes
Las maneras describir deseosos,
Es custumbre a imaginar
Los kilometros a la escuela
Cruzar desmasiados hasta desiertos.
Estrecho durada
En frente del invitarse
A la hora humedo a la luna
Malo a malo el sarape
De pensar perezoso
La nieva en el patio
Satisfecho semana
Solo a sola el sol en la sombra

Si tiene ganas de en el templado temprano.
Ver ultimo trieste
Hace a la revuelta
A la vez y otra vez
A la vida de uva.

7.

Es decir
Que de los simientos
La veras mas verdad
Dibujos son cada propio
La vida esta vivir
En la gente es
ciertos de amor no
Esta en cambio
Porque esta porque,
La lluvia nunca basta
Lluvioso
Como cuanto los anos
Prefieran joven
Poco un poco todo
La tierra no esta
Todavia no todo possible
Proximo querer a resistir
Repetir.

Discipline

The walk to the lake is fourteen city blocks as the crow flies
Taken three miles a week as a discipline
Along broad boulevards with law and medical offices
Across a waking suburb of fountains and small parks,
At seventy one must prepare for eventual restriction
Retire to the balcony at six
For toast and a steep frosted glass of government demitasse
Read the newspaper of the day,
Circle the sheriff night calls,
Not so young but more than twenty-one years passed
When I walked weekends ten miles between five and eight
Swam two miles every morning
Stopped in for tea, cream and fruit at a street café
Or Jewish delicatessen and picked up borscht and veal
Once a month an uphill hike in Briones or Anza Borrego
Several times a year a drive into Death Valley
The Salton Sea surrounded by ethereal windless peaks,

The endless sky is its own plateau
Chalk-gravel ravines streaked by shadow and snow
Miles of sagebrush and wind-blown tumbleweed
Blue from a distance, sparse jade walking through,
One summer I climbed Thor's Canyon
Found my way between sunset-orange, hundred foot rock
Formations as odd as Mono Lake where despite rain
For half the year salt walks with spired hemoglobin,
Daring are the salt boron stretches of California deserts
Painted sands of chocolate and yellow swirls
Devastated reluctant mountains called Old Woman
The breathless air swoops down at ten miles an hour,
Many a year I've stood solitary on a sojourn vista
As though released of humble trials

The stone avenues line up in Monument Valley
All told, cement cracked patterns of a long gone sea
They become abundant in Spring with purple and red
    wildflowers
Where the endless road goes on indefinitely,
I have abandoned my car at Searchlight and at Moab
Beneath the clearest of star studded skies
Until rose sunrise flooded the chalk prairie
Searching for God and answers to the crimes of Loeb,
And traversed high ledges of Zion's stone pools
Beneath her brevity of granite crisscrossed rock face
Climbed the base of El Capitan in autumnal fever
Sparingly lived on beef strips and dried Alaskan salmon
Camped along the creek beds of the American River
Waded in stream flurries and spongy mud sinks
Borrowed of rope to make elevation
By camphor light read Robert Penn Warren inside a tent.
Who knows where shifting sands have made way to,
How many can actually say they've been covered in sand
Like gritty salt that sticks to the skin for weeks
Debases the sense of independence at living in nature,
Where is the mud slopped pants hanging on a clothes line
The silver wildflower stinging nettle
The burnt pans that seared the steak and grits
Where is the compass, the string or the map?
On occasion I rethink this journeying
Into idle spaces and empty regions
Coming home I have often capitulated
The sorrowful hours, the bridle or the bait –
Who leaves, whom can one keep.

Damascus Rose

The darkest mask of the Damascus rose
Fills the softest petals with fragrant knowledge
It is the leather glove-like feel of a wilted collage
Which when pressed between pages of poems stain
Compress Mortal time into a brief refrain
Captures the penury of life-strewn dour
Like ruminations gone madly obsessed,
A strap of deep burgundy velvet a throaty harness knows
With interior gold tithing repressed
Amber rose sculpted soap
Washes away the pride of adorned white gold bracelet
Onslaught of summer heat, rain and beached driftwood
Love finds a wayward path
Through fields of dandelion and leaning birch
Upstairs to the back porch
Where Love listens for the cessation of rain
Watches for a hint of clandestine rays
The sky moves from crimson to purple to grey
Life begins with prairies, hills, winding river follows
Fields of frozen spars, glens with glaciers –
    Whose red door is that
    The only house beyond the trees?
I have lived long beside the wizening swallows
Climbed high above endless plains
Left comfort for a quiet solemn plateau
For lengthy days and longer nights
To recollect love's feverish worth
The promising tumble, the glass of whiskey rye
Early mornings of shadows
Your sweet lime scent of arousal
Of endless hours
Entwined in avowal

As essential as food.
Where has inspiration derived
Pre-dawn frost
Fallen snow or cherry-split forlorned
Laced ponds seen only from a balcony
While staying up late reading Bly;
Who awaits the cultivated theme
The curious husband, the diligent author?
Love interrupts until passions are played out
Then with deliberation beneath the bedroom lamp
The rose petals open, their darkest joy apparent
In stark contrast to muted expressed vows
To shaded observances
Lilac corsage and walnut divinity
To icy plums and green sheen foliage
Through open blinds of windows
Across the dark flowing river
To the snow embankment of white dusted trees.
The bill collector calls at breakfast
While the espresso grows cold
The easel abstract of sienna, burnt orange and red lights
Retreats
Fresh blueberry scones bitten once
Travel is shelved
Snow falls heavily obscuring the snowman
Sunglasses, throng and cruise portfolio
Await another, more opportune
Summer.

www.ingramcontent.com/pod-product-compliance
Lightning Source LLC
Chambersburg PA
CBHW030331080526
44584CB00012B/806